# The Courtesy

Phoenix Poets
*A Series Edited by Robert von Hallberg*

# The Courtesy

*Alan Shapiro*

The University of Chicago Press
*Chicago and London*

Alan Shapiro, lecturer in the
Department of English at Northwestern
University, is the author of *After
the Digging*

The University of Chicago Press, Chicago 60637
The University of Chicago Press, Ltd., London

90 89 88 87 86 85 84 83   5 4 3 2 1

*Library of Congress Cataloging in Publication Data*

Shapiro, Alan, 1952–
   The courtesy.

   (Phoenix poets)
   I. Title.  II. Series
PS3569.H338C6   1983      811'.54      82-24837
ISBN 0-226-75026-4
ISBN 0-226-75027-2 (pbk.)

For my mother and father

Some of these poems first appeared in the following
publications:

*Canto*
*Ploughshares*
*Vanderbilt Poetry Review*
*Pequod*
*The Greensboro Review*
*Cumberland Poetry Review*
*Carolina Quarterly*
*Threepenny Review*
*The Southern Review*
*Occident*
*The Chicago Review*
*The New Republic*
*The American Scholar*
*McCall's*

Special thanks to the Stanford University Creative Writing
Center, where as a Stegner Fellow and Jones Lecturer I had
the time and encouragement to write and revise many of
these poems.

# Contents

# The Host
*(for JM)*

From the curtained light, inside, they must be moving
slowly out of bed, now that I'm here.
However much time has passed since I've been gone
there's never any hurry in their welcome
though they hear the bell. And no reluctance,
for they come in no time, and are always coming,
friends, or lovers, when I am at the door.
I can hear their soft steps over the carpet
and, in that deepening rhythm, I find myself expecting
an unremembered comfort, as though in their approach
all elsewhere goes till I'm almost no where else
but home, and it could be my mother who approaches
when she would find me sleepless at her door,
and till I slept would sing me, Is You Is
Or Is You Ain't My Baby—
                              her song now in the light
that goes on in the hall, the lock that turns.
Even the coldness on my hands and lips turns sweet
because I think whoever finds me here
might find it, at their greeting, a mortal thing.

# The Storm

# On the Eve of the Warsaw Uprising

At the end of the Passover service, a cup of wine is set
aside for the prophet Elijah. The messenger of God, he is
appointed to herald the era of the messiah.

Elijah come in glorious state
For thy glad tidings long we wait.
Ah me, ah me, when cometh he?
Hush! In good time cometh he.

My uncle said, "This is Elijah's wine."
Till then I mimicked listening, wide-eyed
with piety, while underneath the table
I kicked my brother back for kicking me.
The bitter herbs and the unleavened bread
that my uncle said were meant to make me feel
the brick and mortar, and the hurrying
between the walls of water that wind held back—
to me meant only an eternity
of waiting while he prayed, before a meal.

But when that wine was poured, the door left open,
waiting seemed almost holy: a worshipper,
the candle flame bowed in the sudden draft.
And for a moment I thought I'd behold
Elijah's glad lips bend out of the dark
to brighten and drink up into His Light
the Red Sea in the glass
                              that never parted.
For soon my uncle closed the door when we
grew cold, and the flame straightened. "Where was Elijah?"
Nobody in the room had ever asked.

And now I think, knowing what I know,
if anyone had ever come to us,
he could have come only to keep watch
and not to drink; to look upon the glass,
seeing within the wine, as from across
the whole of night, the small flame still as God;
someone who would have known the numberless
doors that have been opened, to be closed;
the numberless who watched till they became
the shimmer in the wine he looked upon.

# Mezuzah

A small case containing a parchment scroll on which a portion of
Deuteronomy is written, attesting to God's everlasting love. It is
said whoever breaks open the Mezuzah and removes the sacred
scroll will incur God's everlasting retribution.

Though unable to imagine
how harm could fit in there,
in that tiny case,
I thought I knew enough
to stay afraid.
       But once,
moving through the quiet house,
I thought, if I can't hear
my own steps, how can God?
And in the laundry room,
by the dryer humming out its heat,
the thick air,
itself, a kind of linen
covering me, unseen,
unnoticed, I knelt down,
and all I was supposed to fear
I crushed
          with my mother's iron.
The little parchment, speckled
with marks too small to read,
fell out. . .
       and nothing happened:
only the washer jerked
into its spin, and made me wait
a little longer

for my blood to turn to salt,
for my hands to wither,
                    for pain.
But nothing happened.
                    And later,
playing with my friends, I knew
there was no mark of Cain
upon my forehead, no
lightning come to split me
like a tree.
            Only something else,
from then on,
wouldn't go away, kept me
up late at night, damaging
my prayers, till even they no longer tamed
the dark
world of my room:
I knew God's wrath, all right,
His retribution coiled,
forever,
in my questioning.

# Heroes

I hear the children warring
all day through the streets, the charm
of their mimic screams, the smokey
bullets rattling from their tongues.
Heroes, all of them, who dive
as they hurl their snow grenades
and, scrambling to their feet, cry
"You're dead! You're dead!" not minding,
really, when those they have killed
keep on running for their lives.

Unless it be this one child
who brings me to the window,
for whom ambush suddenly
became every sound he heard,
anxiety, the barbed wire;
who steps into the open,
his arms raised over his head,
crying his white flag over
and over, "Don't shoot," he pleads,
"don't shoot. I'm already dead."

# The Courtesy

*( for Saul Chessler, 1953–1974)*

I walked from my house down Coolidge Street last night
And air, beginning movement in the trees,
Shook down a hushing from the branches.
On either side of me the houses
Like solid shadow, blocks of silence
In the violet light, so dim without dimming.
And I saw you, Saul, my old friend, waiting
For me at the corner where our two streets met.

I wanted to ask you what it was like to die
But you said first, as if you didn't want to tell me,
"The doctors made me better. We can run again."
You ran behind me (the way you always did),
Your slow strides lunging: though they never could keep up
This time they stayed right there at my heels.
Turning, I saw one pocket inside out
Clapping on your coat front like a white hand.
Your breath quickened, scrawled in the chilling air
Like mine, and vanishing. We ran on a field of snow.
Our footsteps pattered the smooth crust,
Each one feeling like it might break through.
Around us the pure white kindled under violet.

And we returned by train. Sitting next to you,
Staring through the window, I saw your body
Lying like a dark slash in the snow,
Your arms flung up, your legs crossed,
Even as I heard you next to me
Still struggling to catch your breath. You were just
Pretending to be alive—remembering to breathe,
Lumbering under living weight, saying you were cured,
Your flushed cheeks—all just to put me at my ease.
Afraid that your death might embarrass me, even then
Saul, you were more a friend to me than you were dead.
But in my mind the question was still circling:
What is it like to die? But how could I catch you
In a lie which you intended as a kindness?
Beside you on the train, hurtling back
Into the strange familiarity of Coolidge Street,
Remaining silent, I returned the courtesy.

# The Courts at Lawton Street

Soon when the sun drops over the rim
of buildings, across this small tar court
the out of work, the working, students
and dropouts will be running till dark.
But now they are only gathering
in a loose arc before the basket,
in a fog of heat where they forget
what they forget, lazily shooting.

A slow impersonal music winds
through their voices, a great friendliness
so casual nobody needs
to notice; they talk of this and that,
old games, miraculous old moves
only the teller can remember,
though every one of them, agog
with his own miracles, believes.

One hangs back, bouncing in place a ball
others are waiting for him to shoot.
He jitters a little, spins and
pumps as if to shoot, then stands again,
till someone says, "Fuck face, shoot the ball."
Not looking to see if his hook's good,
he waves to the invisible fans
wild with love, cheering him either way.

Now there are three balls, three drab moons
turning through the gold soot of evening,
colliding on the bent rim, making
the metal chain net whisper applause.
At the other end someone dribbles
behind his back, between his legs, while
two small kids chase him till they stumble,
lunging at that ghost between his hands.

And when singing, "Got to sweeten up
my jams" he lopes slowly to the hoop
and stuffs the ball in over his head,
the kids, knowing they watch a god
they could become, with solemnity
slap each other's palms and say, "Nasty,
nasty," as though the word meant only
fame to them, and all there is of hope.

# Sisters

You watch her as through water,
your older sister who must
clean up after you, and cook,
who tells you all the better
things she has to do. Smoking's
all you manage by yourself,
a drifting lifeline that seems
slowly to lift your good hand
up, and let it down. Sometimes,
she catches bright ash burning
in your lap, and sweeps it off
and, where you can't feel, slaps you
till it shames her. She wonders,

sometimes, as she holds you up,
almost pushing you along,
if you are just preferring
these tottering little steps:
"Madam Butterfly, come on."
And though you tell her through the
underwater sounds you make
to go away, she only
takes care then with a vengeance,
as, perhaps, she once took care
to break one of your new toys.
And she is right to do this,

even as you may be right—
to look up through that water
you are falling through, watching
her blurred shape that forces you
to imagine the sharp lines,
the bright air she's speaking from,
that you must sound. You may be
right to want to turn away,
the last way you can hurt her,
free her, turning round to face
that other, purer sister
whose kind dark arms will hold you,
keep you, as they bring you down.

# Someone Else

When she had come to live with them, by then
vanity was all her stroke had left her.
Yet it became another kind of health,
a way to get through days when she would wake
in her wet bed, a child again, afraid
she might be found before the sheets were clean;
or showering, when she would have to see her body
like someone else resisting her, so stiff
it only let her turn enough to reach,
not wash, the bitter smell that clung like shame.

So she would spend the mornings struggling
with her silk slip and dress, and work her stockings
up her legs till they seemed agile with shimmering.
The rouged cheek, the hair done up, the nails
polished till the brightness made her hands
(if only they'd keep still) less like a stranger's—
these enabled her to leave her room
and face them, and believe the care she needed
was what they owed her,
what she permitted them to give. They were,

she would tell herself, tottering her great
weight down the stairs, no better than her husbands,
those first betrayers: the sullen courtesy
her grand child showed, the irritation hiding
in her daughter's pity, she could at least ignore them
(at least there would be power there), and wait
till they went out, wanting them out
so she could feel finally at home,
the t.v. on,
just her and her celebrities.

She could anticipate each set response,
each misery. Nothing could surprise her.
And with a kind of joy she could be certain
that even if some star walked from the screen
the mirror, always at hand, would show her hair
in place, her face powdered; she could feel
the after taste of mouthwash, could even savor
the bitter cleanness in her mouth, and know,
nearly invincible, that she was ready,
should anybody come to take her out.

# Rain

Nobody troubled you
that last night, no one came.
No daughter visited
whose unrelenting care
accused you of your deep
need to have her there:
child then to your own child,
only your needling her
(she could do nothing right)
kept clenched your pride, yet left you
needing her that much more.
Not even your ex-husbands
appeared, as they always did
the moment you were sleeping,
to rummage through your purse
and drawers for every cent
you still imagined yours;
you'd feel their fast hands pass
like shadows over your skin,
still passionate because,
you'd cry, "You bastards can't
forget how good I was."
But seeing no one leave
that night before you woke,
there was, for once, no need
for your complaining, "Go
piss on my back, but don't
tell me it's raining."

                    That night,
all this was past.
                    Mildly,
just to yourself, you spoke
for awhile about the weather
held in your window where,
twenty four years ago,
your stroke had put it:
                    Now
you could hear rain, all right,
outside, troubling you,
though casually, the way
a mother loves small trouble
for the care it lets her show:
mother and child, together—
nobody else was there—
lover and loved, you told
yourself, "Be sure to wear
your coat. It's not that cold
tonight, but you never know.
Be sure to button up
for me, before you go."

# Dancing with Aunt Tilly

One night, one wedding night the band struck up
A song Aunt Tilly used to polka to;
Plump as a lightbulb on its head, she sat
Beside me, old with young, tapping her feet
"The way we used to," tapping louder still
And louder; I saw the music enter at her heels,
Become commotion in her knees, then send
Her sequin dress exploding into stars:
"It's just the two of us!" Then cross the floor
She whirled me till it seemed our ages met,
My small feet followed four steps to her one.

Later, beyond the fear she squeezed me in,
Her breasts embraced my ears and made
My head a bug between two mountains;
After it no longer seemed I'd suffocate
Because she lost her breath and let me go,
I felt the pleasure that a fear can leave:
A map of jewelry throbbed on my hot cheeks,
Everywhere old polka songs kept on and on,
And, hardly tapping either foot, she sat
As if her sitting was a dance too much.

# Simon, the Barber

It seemed I was your only customer,
yet too much work whenever I came in:
the barbershop's suspicious hairlessness;
the only sign of life, the front door bell
ringing you out of sleep in the big chair;
the ceiling light glowing like a bright coin
on your bald head. As if I had intruded,
you'd get up slow, resentful, mumbling
"So? Vhat kind of haircut? I haven't got all day."
Yet everytime you'd have to test me first
as if to prove, before you'd cut my hair,
that I was still a Jew, making me read
from the Yiddish papers scattered through the shop,
telling me who the goyim were: "Jew haters,
remember. God forbid you should forget."
And when you'd, finally, give me the same trim,
no matter what my mother said to say,
you wouldn't touch my sideburns. So later on
she'd have to cut them off.

                    Turning the chair
this way and that, you would—just like Matisse
who never lifted pencil from the page—
keep clipping constantly from ear to ear,
pointing me in the chair around the shop:
I'd see the other chairs, the leather cushions
smooth and forbidden like museum furniture;
the glass case by the front door always holding
a rainbow of elixirs, tonics, creams,
"Medicine for longer lasting hair"
the labels, scrawled in your long hand, read. You'd say,
"See," tilting the smooth, bright surface of your head,
"Vhat happens, Mr. Big Shot, vit out medicine."
And then you'd turn me toward the dreaded window
where often friends would pass, jeering at me
in the white cape, one ear lower than the other:
"Bums" is all you'd say and swing me round
to face the door that opened to your flat—
sometimes hearing the not so muffled sounds
of fighting in the next room, you would give
your shoulders a slight shrug, as if to say
"So? Vhat did you expect, Joy?"

As years went by
I saw you less and less, my hair each time
a little longer, my sideburns secular;
dressed up like the goyim in bright colors
you, and your law, no longer mine, could bless.
And the last time you agreed to cut my hair
(For after that it was, "I vouldn't cut
that head vit a lawnmower") you asked me,
"So, Mr. Beatnik, vhat do you vant to do
vitch your life?"
                    "I'd like to teach, I guess."
"That's good," you answered, "teaching you'll make enough."
"But making enough's not what I want from life."
"Then be a lawyer," you replied, triumphant,
"you'll make more than enough!"
                                    Around that time,
I read about your son, who was my age,
arrested in a drug raid. And I recall
the deadly irony in your raised eyes
whenever you would see me, or my kind.
From then on, once again, you were surrounded
by enemies more dangerous than any
you had fled—your children, your own seed;
all that you had suffered and survived
and learned, mere ashes in our prayer for the dead.

Yet, now, I thank you for this legacy
and know that you would never take my thanks.
Your earned disdain is all I can expect.
Still, I would greet you, if I had the chance,
though you would pass, and never turn your head;
still I would greet you, Sir, across the years
as an old enemy to an old friend.

# Milking

*( for my father)*

**1**

The bucket banging
hollow sounds out on my knees
down the back porch stairs
across hard snow
on Hill's Field where I was walking
towards the barn floating half in night.
Inside I knew
the dark cows waited,
lugging out their long dense calls.

**2**

Entering, I saw them
shifting in their stalls; I heard
hoofs knocking and the softer sounds
of dung
dropping to the floor—

I beat my bucket with a stick
and, rumbling, the cows
shook loose
from the deepest parts
the long, slow, letting down
of milk.

**3**

I slapped a wet cloth on
the heavy bag; washed off dried bits
of dung and mud; my fingertips
touching the firm plump give
made me forget, almost, the chores
I'd have to do;

and I shoved my shoulder
under her right thigh, dug in against her
kick, dug in till her switch
whipped my neck; and,
leaning forward, my forehead pressing
on the scratchy flank,

I reached in for the teats.
Feeling them filling as they emptied out,
I pulled and squeezed, my fingers
hardly mine
so completely rhythm,
and every muscle in my arms

as tight as stone,
with one hand stripping, the other
letting go, my fingers down
and down again,
while in the bucket the tin rang
to the milk's hot hiss.

**4**

Holding the wire handle with both hands,
I paused once at the door,
and saw the sun's face, barely lifted,
make Hill's Field burst up to my narrowed eyes;
and as I walked out into that brightness, that
trembling of snow about to melt,
and the brightness in my bucket
splashing my clenched hands,
I knew, behind me, the cows were quiet,
lying down into the last dark places
of the before dawn darkened barn.

# Perfect Son

Your father stands with you there, his face clouded
to untouchable indifference above the dark suit,
mere life in his eyes. Old age tenders him
to you, it holds his arm around your waist,
the large hand you fear now more than ever
gently to your hip. It is his weakness
comes to love you (your arm circling his shoulder),
that seems to hold you up. Yet smiling eagerly,
anxious for the shutter to close on this one
gift, so much your own it makes you fear
he'll take it back, you look as though,
tense with too much privilege, you could see
his rightful son ready to step into the frame.

You can say your father loved you now
and so forget how long you had to labor
to believe this, how long before you learned to love
your fear of him. At home, in the slaughterhouse,
the knife of his devouring "Thou Shalt Not"
cut and shaped you on the block of need,
his second son who never would come first.
When you knew the rage he showed you was your own
unworthiness, you wanted to be nothing
but your father's son. And seeing this,
he could pull out that blade, sheer law,
and know you happily would cling to it.

You would like to think this picture heals you,
sitting before it on these nights when sleep,
—fathering now, aloof and unappeasable—
refuses you. But he will not say
again what you have done, how you offended.
Even now, he gives you only your sharp need
to please him, never to disappoint him, his death
your final punishment. Like a small boy
up past his bedtime, you must hear downstairs
everything your denial has awakened,
the wide strap slapping his palm as he mounts the stairs
and calls you in your own voice now, angry,
your perfect father calling for his perfect son.

# Yahrzeit

Each year my father has another soul
to pray for, another anniversary
of another's death, someone else to love
belatedly. Today it's his brother,
Amos, who died hating him and being hated.
Still my father stands here
bent over the little candle flame, swaying.
He can feel the old estrangements, the golden calf
of grievances their anger forged and worshipped
softening in these words, melting at last
to this barely articulated rise and fall,
more moan than prayer. It's as though his own loss,
his real brother, had become the wick
of this anonymous, inextinguishable sorrowing
whose pure heat, burning what he knows,
gives back to him unhindered love, another
family, a brother who can hear him now
and would have prayed for him, and loved him
as he never did, as his brother's brother
here in these syllables, if no where else.

# After the Storm

The others were still sleeping in the house.
And here the quiet was as if all sound

Were just beyond the edge of hearing, on
The point of being heard. Snow crashing softly

From somewhere off a roof, a high-pitched humming
In your ears, growing fainter and more tense.

You were between belonging anywhere:
Pausing in space between pulsebeats, and cold,

And unaware of any pain, your mind
As trackless as the surface of white shapes;

Yourself only a surface, with perceptions
Just resting on your eyes, no further in:

You watched your breath print whiteness in the air,
Vanishing without a trace. And walked,

A darker crystal than the crust that held,
A momentary plunging through white earth.

# Crossing

# What Makes You Think It's Fear

Each morning from the house he sees the cat
who won't come near him, entering the garden.
It moves along the fencetop, through the ivy,
making the sounds of someone keeping quiet,
making him listen.
            He wonders what it fears:
what makes it leap away when he goes out—
to perch on the far corner of the fence,
its paws drawn under it, the tail pulled round
like a moat?
            In time the cat will stay, he thinks,
in time learn how mistaken its fears are.
He brings an offering to prove he's kind,
holding out to it a bowl of food,
shaking the bowl to prove that it is full
and not a trap,
                calling out sweet names.
But far into the leaves the cat retreats
before it disappears; its green eyes glaring
and yet with no alarm, as he approaches,
holding the bowl and, almost fearful,
                            calling,
calling out as if he asks for alms.

# The Insect

There is someone sleeping on the couch.
The radio on the floor is on

with no volume like someone talking
to himself—each tube shines and flickers

incommunicable energy.
There is someone sleeping on the couch.

On the table in half-filled cups
coffee stiffens to a black mirror

giving back the light three times. The same
light vibrates in the fine snow

in the sugarbowl, glints off
the kettle, shakes like a drop

of fire in the teaspoon's hand.
Someone is sleeping on the couch and

is about to stir. For the last time
in the room just an insect budges

the mile of inches across the table,
between the unexplainable arrangement

of megalithic breadcrumbs, past the cups,
the sugarbowl, the kettle's

ungraspable structure, while the sleeper goes
on sleeping on the couch, and the earth

angles sunlight through the window above his head,
through which the tiny knocking together of dust

drops into nothing. It is so quiet
a black cat might be walking

but just the insect's minute purpose
and particles of dust move

where the sleeper, about to stir, is balanced
on the vanishing edge between this moment

and the next, before the rapid
flashing of his dream begins

to signal in the afternoon that
he is someone sleeping on the couch,

no longer undeniably part
of things, like the insect, the half-filled

cups, the radio talking to itself, or
someone sleeping on the couch about to stir.

# First Night

If not relaxed that night,
we were, at least, not quite
that nervous; awkward, yes,
yet our uneasiness
became a kind of ease:
the way rain in the trees,
after a rain, is kept
by each impediment
from falling, as it falls.
So we'd advance, and stall,
fearing to show off, or
wishing we'd offered more—
until each courtesy
of pleasure let us see
how easy it is to praise
touching in all our ways:
with great or no aplomb,
with old hands, or all thumbs.

# In the Neighborhood

Along the little alley between the backs
of close-set separate houses and backyards,
the trees rise up into each other's branches,
forming on either side another hedge
over the leafless hedges, and over me
as I walk home late in the afternoon.
Here and there, a house light in the hedge
breaks into several lights, or holds a woman
like a picture of a woman sitting—
she's probably the mother of this child
who bends, fetching the ball a friend has thrown.
Though the sky darkens, and soon she'll call him in,
he pauses by the thick mesh of branches,
the ball in one hand, and his friend behind him,
and, behind his friend, inside the house, his mother.
Held fast to what he knows, he watches me
as I flick past, only a strange man passing:
Does he imagine I see him there and wonder
why I'm his neighbor only, and not him? . . . .

Safe in my father's bed on Sunday mornings,
he used to tell us how, if we weren't good,
the neighbors would come get us in the night
and take us to their houses and make us live there.
Hiding under his sheets, I knew that goodness
was his warm bed, the thigh I lay against.
I pictured the cold terror of those rooms
next door, thinking that 'neighbor' meant the same
as banishment, an unfamilied captivity—
it was what would happen when you died:
you passed on into your neighbors' houses,
and neighbors would be where your parents were,
and you lived with them forever. . . . I smile at the boy
and he runs away. Yet as I reach my door
I keep in mind this brief coincidence
that I'll forget, and surely have again,
because, however briefly, it can chasten
with ordinary strangeness, theirs and mine.
It may be, even now, a chancy goodness
that someone passing sees my light go on
and thinks, at one more square of light,
that a neighbor whom he doesn't know is home.

# Certain Healing

You and I have seen
sometimes the wounded
animal, who must
instinctively keep
circling back, and
back across the bright
emptiness of snow,
to the thicket, dark
and hidden; where, poised
in pain, it must see
all help approaching
as the same danger.

But what risk have we
come to now, who must
keep circling back
and back into this
covert of ourselves,
holding only to
our own pain; who know
what help is out there
waiting, yet still choose
to hide in this ice-
hard and, so we think,
more certain healing?

# The Source

As we start over, patience
Is the calm source I will need.

And I will have to find it
Here in our inclemencies,

When the hard rain or thick snow
Obscures us, and I wonder

(As I always did before)
If it could be mere weather.

Now patience must be, at worst,
Our intimate denial

Of the unfed, angry child;
At best, the random clearing

Where we pause, though no less hurt,
With light, alone, between us.

All we need to do is see
That light, and we are drinking

Together at that cold spring
Hidden somewhere in our thirst.

# Love Letter

Today, a soft rain
brings all outside near:
clear globes blur the trees
to a green atmosphere.

Evening lasts all day.
And through the house some
power comes, aimless,
calm, and you become

altered, a woman
I no longer know,
whom I may guess at,
whose attractions grow

as you grow more vague.
In this weather there's
something I should fear,
but can't; this rain stirs,

bringing its dark haze
down through trees; through me
darkening into
safe obscurity,

till even thoughts of you,
your hands' kind gestures,
seem like commands, your
softest touch, pressure

I can't bear. Feeling
just self-regard, and,
unafraid, I'm scared:
Dear, when will this end?

this rain chilling me?
Bring love's hard light home—
come back to where I,
knowing you, am known.

# Only Then

I have to tell you:
last night, as you lay
next to me, the tree
at our window grew
farther from us than
any distance. You

were sleeping, still and
curved as a snowdrift,
your breath slowing to
a soft tide; while I,
fool worrier I am,
got beyond, for once,

the restlessness, the
needing to hold fast
to joy, that only
holds joy from me. I
need to tell you how
last night I touched you

easily, and you,
unaware, turned back
as if in welcome,
as if I'd been gone
a long time, and had,
only then, come home.

# Conscience

Through the window, in the wide night sky alone,
Old Mother, I feel your presence now, as always,
your blank consideration looking on
like conscience, when I am happiest.
In your ample light of otherwise and elsewhere,
as her head rests on my arm, you cast
arm and head alike into a life
that's never good enough. For nothing, you have taught me,
is too good for your son. Even her touch, asleep,
you can turn to my desire for perfection
which only you can satisfy. You numb
the arm that holds her, and you keep it there,
holding the blanket to her shoulder so she won't need
to stir, providing with cool diligence
the proper warmth. Though I grow cold,
coldness will be my secret, and my power;
it's how eventually I'll free myself,
how I am free of her already
awake in the heatless light of your devotion,
the chaste freedom you alone can give.

# Escape Artist

Elusive as Houdini, the way he steals
into another's heart, beyond all doubt:
then goes to work, the only prop he needs
the reason he can find for getting out.

The times he's suffered from some small offense
which he would never mention, or forget;
the daily quarrels, unreasonable demands;
these ease his getaway, and his regret.

Besides, we're all artists when it comes to this—
he thinks he's simply better than the rest:
leaving sometimes before there's reason to,
knowing enough to leave before he's left.

And yet he's often scared by his success:
at night when he's, himself, the lidless box,
hearing a stranger's voice, "Get out of this,
get out of this," his heart clicking like a lock.

But that is just the hazard of a trade
and, once learned, is as hard to put aside
as a strait jacket; one he can't escape,
this skill at getting free which keeps him tied.

# Moving Day

Moving the furniture—
last relics of what they
together had arranged—
outside, out of the way,
he finds, because familiar,
the house becoming strange.

He rubs from bare white walls
the fog of webs, the scuff
of insects that he killed
and left, that added up
as if a kind of scrawl
whose meaning he now stills.

So cleaning house becomes
forgetting, as he cleans;
a covering of tracks
in an otherworldly gleam,
when no one's ever come,
where nothing stains, or cracks;

where perfect, for a time,
each sound inhabits quiet—
the dust is light that rains,
and hangers from the closet
chime from across a distance
no house could contain.

# Harvesting

We watched the lemons through the spring and summer,
small planets turning out of their green night
so slowly that we knew it would be winter
before we'd gather in that yellow light.

And, unaware, we shared as slow a ripening.
As quietly as lemons turning color,
our sweet days turned into remembering,
too swift a fragrance at the edge of anger.

And though it's winter and in the garden now
the lemons hang like worlds, forever day
for someone else, what weighed on other boughs
we harvest separately, and take away.

# Fossils

The fossils of the warm
bright sunlight of the year
flicker from these dry leaves
falling through the garden air.

And we who would find comfort
in shards we might retrieve,
find—whirling at our feet
out of a sky of leaves—

past days are no less past:
however near they are,
they touch us with the bright,
cold comfort of the stars.

# The Garden

Sleepless, I'm unable not to hear the stories
sliding like night creatures from everything
I remember only now. Hungry
for whatever gets them told, they feed
when the leg twitches, at the sudden jag of the heart.
They grow alert with what comes and goes,
the slightest hurrying: mice in the darkest places,
squirrels running nervously across the roof.
Each plane, as it crosses my hearing, articulates their speech
till I am there, some passenger (a small child in his lap)
thinking of whatever can go wrong.

I think of them, crouched in The Garden
behind the thickest trees, hiding
for the first time ever, though not from God,
unable not to know the sound their minds made
sliding through everything they saw: the trees
all suddenly restless, and the bright fruit
flashing everywhere, out of the dark leaves telling
what they had done, what they would do.

# The Crossing

How long since I made this crossing on some good dream?
Not like today, waking where I read
by the lamplight now brighter than the sun,
showing me the shadow of my head on the pillow.
Who was it, years ago, would wake me so gradually
that waking was another falling back to sleep;
whose smile nurtured me in ways I never needed
till they were mine, a having that had no wanting first?
There were all those leaves then (and birds within those
    leaves)
crossing the pillow as my eyes opened,
moving this way and that across my brother
next to me, along my arm. Alone,
before anyone woke, I remember how
needlessly happy I could be, how needlessly at home.

# Fly Weight

Another morning I wake up with a headache,
needing aspirin and coffee, needing to think
"At least, today, I don't have to leave the house."
"At least," my morning hymn, my passwords
through the infinite regress of making do
with little, and less, until making do becomes
a lesson I've learned too well, a weightless cherishing.
Taking the wrong thing because I couldn't notice,
leaving behind the right, is currency by now,
a kind of money in my kind of bank.
Sluggish, achey, I get up like a fighter
from one too many eight counts, unaware
of who it is he fights; knowing only
that his head aches, that he is fighting, that something's wrong.

# Counting Flowers

Only a few posters on the walls to tame
the rented beast, some used furniture, books,
no pets or plants I'd only have to give away;
I am orderly by circumstance: a cup and two dishes
in the sink, together with the pot and pan;
and two drawers for my clothes, though both are full,
too full to close, like bags I'm on a bad day packing,
unpacking on a good. On the road, even at home,
my most secure belongings are the backward glance
and the unforeseen; happiest in one place
the moment I can think I'm leaving,
cleaning up a little, throwing things away.

# Within the Room

Always you feel the change too late
when there is nothing you can do,
when with the subtlety of weather
living becomes a living through.

Through all your disciplined distractions—
the whiskey's rigid warmth, t.v.,
the letters that you try to write,
and books—a kind of clarity

bleakens your senses as it falls,
until a voice, like yours, is talking,
saying: it's distances within
the room that snow, that keep you walking—

as if each distance were a sin
for which this walking could atone;
says hell's the gesture of a prayer
when you kneel down beside the phone

and dial, and listen; and when you know
that there is no one answering,
when no one's home, it says: don't ever
put the phone down—let it ring.

# The Clearing

Your dinner over, too tired to read or write,
fatigue makes you remember that you can't sleep.
You clear the table. And wiping it till your face
shines back, you read there too easily
the moral of some wrong turn. Too easily you hear
those hounds of significance, wildly flushing
out into this clearing, like some prize game,
all the elusive sadnesses, fugitive regrets.
Let them go tonight. Not so predictable, or coy,
mice drawn in by the warmth are running
through the cupboards like far away deer,
gathering wood chips and bits of things to soften
the floor of cups and small bowls where they will sleep.
You have whiskey's honey light for warmth,
for illumination if you're lucky;
and there's good company on the radio,
a woman singing in—Italian, or is it Spanish?
You can tell what she sings is intimate,
though not meant for you; it's no less yours.
Accept it.
               What more could you ask for now
than this sweet voice, this gratitude?

# Song for a Time of Year

Now when the leaves
come down in a flash
flood through the trees,
with a soft crash;

when one by one
what you would hold
goes from you, come,
come out of the cold.

Call home your caring
from not enough
and too much daring;
for once, give up

what can't be won—
before you find
all love withdrawn,
leave love behind.

Take now what rest
may still survive
what you must miss,
what you're denied,

and start to learn:
seeking desire
in wood that burns,
and not in fire.

# Long Days

These are the long days when
the sunlight breathes
out of the shadows on the ground
and into leaves;

days when the air is nervous
with the sound of birds;
when through the trees from other gardens
the faintest words—

fragrant with all distance—
come to your ear:
each one, a wish that vanishes
before you hear;

each one reminding you
you must beware:
when all you've ever wished for comes
to all you are.

# The Wish

That day the late sun, wrinkling on the pond,
drew shadows of bright water up the sycamore.
You and your daughter played. And as I looked on
I could see faint currents, as if within the water,
roll up through the breezeless air, across the leaves,
setting adrift the stiffest branches, rippling
the smooth trunk; it was as if the water dreamed
it was a tree even a small stone could scatter.

You and your daughter were running in that dream
in a widening circle, happier than I
had ever seen you, your voices a single sound.
How clearly I saw, then, those delicately shifting lights
between you, while I stood at the edge; how well
I knew, watching you entering each other's arms,
that I should not call, should not even want
to join you in that seamlessness, too much
your own and hers, even for that wish, this stone.

# The Names
*( for Ken and Nora)*

Intimacy means the names of trees.
And, walking in these hills you know so well,
this new terrain for me, you give the names
of Willow, Pine and Buckeye, and the bright
torrent, the Liquid Amber leaves. Your voices
enter a faint excitement in the air,
a scattering of sparrows: like leaves ascending
from a Live Oak, whose name approaches me
more natural than the flight of birds. Yet all
I think I will remember is the Greasewood—
under which we found where deer had rested
just hours before, the shadow of their weight
still on the grass,
                    so delicate an absence.
But, hesitant as squirrels our walking scares,
the names emerge, Madrone, Acacia, Fir,
emerging over an uncertain ground,
at a slow pace, this fellowship of names,
this way of speaking I am slow to learn.
I fear an inexactness in the sounds,
of moving too close, or never close enough;
I lag behind you, trying to repeat
the names to myself first, and then to you,
wanting, too much, to make a perfect giving
for everything I have received:

                    Dear Friends,
forgive me the good distance of my tact,
think it makes coming to you possible,
a way of meeting, not of holding back:
though I hold back, still when you see me think
that I am someone learning how to swim,
testing the water, careful, going out
slowly, and back, and out a little farther
toward where you are, who call my name:
                                        Believe
I'm coming, even though I strain to keep,
as long as I can, one toe to the sand.